C000044671

Nature's Window

BEARS

Nature's Window

BEARS

Sheila Buff

ANDREWS AND MCMEEL

A UNIVERSAL PRESS SYNDICATE COMPANY

KANSAS CITY

Introduction

The bear has a very special place in human culture. Venerated for its strength and wisdom, it is also feared for its ferocity. In some societies, warriors wore bearskins into battle to project ferocity. The ancient Greeks saw the Great Bear and the Little Bear in the constellations we call the Big and Little Dippers. For many, a bear's hibernation and spring reappearance,

A polar bear standing erect easily reaches the awesome height of ten feet. Standing upright gives the bears a good view of the terrain. With their good eyesight, bears can see for a mile.

often with newborn cubs, is seen as a symbol of

resurrection and renewal. In some Native American

cultures, the bear is seen as a wise and powerful

Even when they are alone, polar bears play. Here a bear amuses itself by rolling on the ice. elder brother; the Inuit people of the

Arctic attribute supernatural powers to the

polar bear. In American society, until this century the bear symbolized danger lurking in the woods, but today the bear represents the modern conservation ethic. In all cultures, the bear is seen as a powerful symbol of the wild.

This cuddly-looking polar bear weighs nearly a thousand pounds; its paws can be twelve inches in diameter.

THE BEAR FAMILY

Of the eight different species of bears, three of the most common are found in North America: black bears, brown bears, and polar bears. The most numerous and widespread of these are black bears, which are found only in North America. They live wherever there is forested land, from northern Canada into the mountains of Mexico, and from California to Florida.

The name black bear is a little misleading, for these animals actually range in color from

Black bears can range in color from deep black to almost white. Many, but not all, have a distinctive lighter-colored muzzle. At the shoulder, a typical black bear stands between three and four feet tall.

creamy white to cinnamon brown to dark black. Ranging from three to four feet tall at the shoulder, the black bear is the smallest North American bear, but when it stands on its hind legs it can be as tall as six feet. Their weight can range from 150 to more than 600 pounds.

Brown bears, also known as grizzlies, are found across much of the northern hemisphere, including the Arctic regions of North America, Europe (where it is the only bear), Asia, and into the heavily forested subarctic regions of Alaska, Canada, Siberia, and northern China.

Like black bears, brown bears vary greatly in color, ranging from tan to deep brown to almost black. The name *grizzly* is often applied to all brown bears, but it really should be used to refer only to the brown bear, found in the interior forests of North America, whose fur is dark and tipped with shimmery silver-colored hairs, giving it a "grizzled" appearance.

Brown bears are considerably larger than black bears; they have much longer claws and a distinct shoulder hump. A typical male grizzly weighs more than a

Once they leave their mothers at the age of two or three, brown bears lead solitary lives. They usually come together only occasionally at rich, seasonal food sources such as salmon streams. Even at such times, the bears keep a respectful distance from each other to avoid conflict. When they come face to face, the encounter is cautious. One bear is generally clearly subordinate to the other, but sometimes equals meet. The ensuing tussle may be fierce, but the loser is usually not seriously hurt.

thousand pounds and can be eight feet tall when he stands erect. Despite their size, these animals can run at speeds reaching forty miles per hour.

Polar bears are the largest members of the bear family. These massive animals, found only in the icy Arctic region, are closely related to the brown bears. A typical male polar bear weighs about twelve hundred pounds and stands well over ten feet tall. The largest polar bear on record weighed more than two thousand pounds and was over twelve feet tall. Polar bears are always a creamy white color, with huge paws and a short tail. They are very powerful swimmers, with extremely strong back legs and partially webbed paws. A polar bear can swim in icy Arctic waters for more than fifty miles without stopping, and researchers have spotted the bears on ice floes more than two hundred miles from shore.

The Asian black bear, also called the moon bear because of the crescent-shaped white mark on its chest, is a close cousin of the North American bears. About the size of a black bear, the moon bear is found in rugged areas of central Asia, including Iran, Afghanistan, northern Pakistan, and the forested areas of Manchuria and central China. Moon bears are notoriously bad-tempered, so little is known of their life cycle. However, because moon bears walk upright very well, they are often captured as cubs and trained to perform circus tricks.

Three bear species live quite close to the equator and are often called "tropical" bears. The sun bear is a resident of the Malay region, including the jungle islands of Java, Sumatra, and Borneo

The sun bear gets its name from the yellowish crescent on its chest. Sun bears spend their days lounging and sleeping in tree nests and their nights foraging for food in their jungle habitat.

and the mainland of the Malay Peninsula and Myanmar; it is also found in some densely forested parts of India. Weighing only about one hundred pounds, the sun bear is by far the smallest member of the bear family.

The sloth bear, found in the forests of Sri Lanka, India, and Nepal, is perhaps the most unusual bear. It has a long, black, shaggy coat with a large, white, chevron-shaped blaze on its chest. A typical sloth bear stands six feet tall and weighs about three hundred pounds. This unique bear has very long, powerful claws on its front feet and a long, flexible muzzle. The sloth bear rips open termite mounds and ant nests with its claws and sucks up insects with its almost toothless muzzle.

The spectacled bear, the only species in South America, is found only in the Andes Mountains from Venezuela to Chile. This short-muzzled, fairly large bear gets it name from the light-colored rings around its eyes, which resemble eyeglasses. The spectacled bear is an excellent climber and spends a lot of time up in trees, where it feeds almost entirely on leaves and fruit.

Spectacled bears are generally found in trees. These bears very rarely eat meat, sticking instead to vegetarian foods such as corn, sugar cane, honey, and fruit. Spectacled bears have powerful jaws and a rugged digestive system that allows them to eat very coarse plant foods, such as spiny leaves, cactus plants, tough roots, and palm nuts, which other animals can't chew.

Eating like a Bear

Bears are members of the large family Carnivora (meat-eating animals), but meat actually makes up only a small part of their usual diet. In fact, black bears and grizzly bears exist mostly on plants, although they will eat any sort of animal, including small rodents and fish, if they don't have to work too hard to catch it. In Alaska, when salmon come together in large numbers to spawn, bears gather to feed on them, catching the fish in their mouths or flipping them out of

To catch a fish, brown bears usually wade right into the water and seize the fish in their mouths or flip it out of the water with a paw. Bears consider the skin of the fish the best part.

the water with a paw. Polar bears are much more carnivorous, eating seals whenever possible, yet they often eat kelp, grass, berries, and other vegetables.

Bears are omnivores—they will eat almost anything. Their favorite foods include grasses, nuts, berries, seeds, dandelions, honey, fish, carrion, and insects. But they do not limit themselves to food found in the wild. Bears often congregate at garbage dumps to eat the scraps humans discard and sometimes become beggars or thieves at campgrounds.

Although the individual hairs are clear, a polar bear's fur appears white because it reflects the light. The bear's skin, which is black, absorbs heat, helping to keep it warm as it stands on ice floes looking for seals.

Rich food sources such
as salmon runs are
very attractive to all
bears. Here a family
group consisting of a
mother grizzly bear
and three half-grown
cubs feasts on salmon
at a river's edge.

A bear's digestive system is not particularly well designed for a diet that consists largely of plant foods. Food moves so rapidly through a bear that much of it goes undigested. For this reason, bears have huge appetites and spend almost the whole of every day looking for food and eating it. They especially like foods that are high in fat, such as nuts. A polar bear often eats only a seal's fat-rich skin and the thick layer of fat or blubber just below it, leaving the meat for other scavengers such as gulls and Arctic foxes.

Despite their fearsome reputation, brown bears are chiefly vegetarians. Berries and fruits of all sorts are among their favorite foods, but they also eat other plant foods such as leaves, roots, acorns, and even grass.

HIBERNATION

One reason black and brown bears eat so much is that they must build up enough fat reserves during the long summer days to see them through the winter. As the cold weather approaches and food supplies dwindle, these bears seek out a sheltered den such as a shallow cave, a large hollow log, or a burrow dug into the earth and line it with dried leaves or grass. Here they will hibernate for the next three to six months, until spring arrives. During hibernation, bears sleep

A grizzly bear's long claws distinguish it from its close cousin the black bear. Ferocious as they look, the claws are only rarely used as a weapon. They are used to dig up roots and bulbs for food.

deeply, although they can also be easily awakened by an animal or human trying to enter their den. They don't eat, drink, or eliminate, and their heartbeats slow from a normal forty to fifty beats per minute to just eight or ten. Researchers are still exploring the reasons for the bears' physiological changes during hibernation.

Polar bears don't hibernate in the usual manner. Instead, they sometimes den for a few weeks in the middle of summer in cool burrows dug into the permafrost, the permanently frozen layer below the surface. Polar bears are actually most active in the winter when hunting for their preferred food, seal, is easiest. To catch a seal, a bear lurks near a seal's breathing hole in the ice and seizes it when it comes up for air. The Arctic seas are covered with ice that extends for hundreds of miles in winter, allowing the bears more opportunity to catch seals during those months. During the ice-free summer months, polar bears disperse across the Arctic tundra. In late autumn, they migrate back to coastal areas such as Churchill in Manitoba on Hudson Bay to wait for winter ice to form.

BEAR CUBS

Bears become sexually mature at about five to six years of age. They mate in the late spring or early summer, but the fertilized eggs enter a sort of suspended animation until the female bear dens for the winter. Then, depending on how large her fat reserves are, anywhere from one to four of the eggs implant in her womb and start to grow.

Two American black bear cubs in their preferred habitat: a combination of woodlands and open areas. This terrain can be found in the hardwood forests of the East and the conifer forests of the West.

Usually, just two cubs are born; if the female doesn't have enough reserves, she will have no cubs at all. Pregnancy, birth, and about the

first month or so of the cubs' lives take place while the
mother bear is hibernating.

Although polar bears don't normally hibernate,
pregnant females do. They dig chambers or dens into a
snowbank in October or November and give birth to
their cubs in December or January. The tiny cubs remain
in the den until the long winter nights give way to more
abundant sunshine in the early spring.

A female polar bear has one to four cubs, although twins are most common. The cubs will nurse until they are almost two years old. By age three, most young bears are ready to leave the family group.

Pregnancy in a bear lasts only about six to eight
weeks. Baby bears are very small and helpless

when they are born. A newborn brown bear, for example, weighs only about ten ounces, while its mother may weigh more than four hundred pounds. Baby bears grow rapidly in the warm shelter of the den, however, and are ready to accompany their mother when the warm weather arrives. They usually go everywhere with her, learning how to forage for food and avoid danger. The cubs even go into the water with their mother. When mother polar bears go swimming, their cubs ride piggyback.

Mother bears are very protective of their cubs; the

father bear has nothing to do with raising them. The biggest danger to bear cubs is aggressive male bears who often try to kill them. When the cubs are threatened, they may climb up into the nearest tree for protection.

Bear cubs stay with their mother for two to three years. They can then fend for themselves in the wild, and their mother will chase them away and mate again. Bear siblings often stay together for several years after their mother has chased them away. Once they reach maturity, though, bears are basically solitary animals.

CONSERVATION

Despite their reputation for ferocity, bears attack humans very rarely. There are no more than a handful of attacks a year in North America, and most of these occur when a female with cubs is surprised or threatened. Bears much prefer to simply avoid humans. We, on the other hand, have hunted bears for centuries.

Due to hunting and habitat loss, by 1900, black bears had been almost eliminated from the eastern half of the United States. In the

As adults, brown bears occasionally climb trees in search of food but cubs climb trees more often, to look for food, to escape predators such as wolves, and frequently just for the fun of it.

1940s, conservation efforts began to save the remaining population and today the total North American population is somewhere between 300,000 and 750,000. Black bears are doing reasonably well in the East, especially in Pennsylvania and in Maine. In the western part of the country, black bears were never so greatly reduced in number; Washington and Oregon have large populations.

The large numbers may be deceiving, however. Habitat loss as woods are cut down, along with hunting and a growing black market for bear parts (gallbladders,

paws, and fat are used in traditional Chinese medicine)
are very serious threats to black bears.

Grizzlies too are seriously threatened by habitat loss
and human hunting. When European settlers arrived in
North America, there were probably about half a million
grizzly bears roaming the land. Today there are fewer
than one hundred thousand. About twenty thousand of
these are found in Alaska, with almost all the rest in the
Yukon Territory and the Canadian Rockies region.
Though its presence was once so common in California

A grizzly bear takes a break from fishing near a salmon river in Alaska. In the space of an hour a grizzly bear can easily catch and eat a dozen salmon. On such an abundant diet, the bear can gain up to six pounds of fat in a single day.

that its likeness is part of the state flag, grizzly bears have been extinct in that state for decades.

The worldwide population of polar bears is probably about fifteen thousand. The population seems to have been quite stable for the past century or more, but even polar bears, in their remote and inhospitable habitat, have been affected by habitat destruction. Oil exploration, hydroelectric projects, and even tourists eager to photograph the polar bears may be putting extra pressure on their environment and lowering their reproductive rate.

In 1902, President Theodore Roosevelt, the founder of the American conservation movement, was on a hunting trip in the South. His hosts had trapped a bear cub for him to kill, but Roosevelt angrily refused to shoot the helpless animal. The publicity surrounding the incident inspired the invention of the teddy bear, which has become the world's favorite stuffed animal. Nearly a century later, the conservation ethic that created the teddy bear is needed more than ever to help keep real bears alive in their wilderness homes.

Photography credits
All images provided by Ellis Nature Photography
©Gerry Ellis: pages 2, 4, 9, 12-13, 17, 20-21, 22, 26-27, 31, 44-45
©Walt Enders: pages 6-7, 25, 28, 35, 37
©Konrad Wothe: page 40
Front jacket: ©Gerry Ellis
Back jacket: ©Walt Enders

ISBN: 0-8362-2782-4

Printed in Hong Kong

First U.S. edition

1   3   5   7   9   10   8   6   4   2

Editor: Linda Hetzer
Art director: Susi Oberhelman
Designer: Yolanda Monteza

Produced by Smallwood and Stewart, Inc., New York City